D0876075

"I Don't Care!"
LEARNING ABOUT RESPECT
Brian Moses and Mike Gordon

WAYLAND

The VALUES series:

"EXCUSE ME" LEARNING ABOUT **POLITENESS**
"I DON'T CARE!" LEARNING ABOUT **RESPECT**
"I'LL DO IT!" TAKING **RESPONSIBILITY**
"IT WASN'T ME!" LEARNING ABOUT **HONESTY**

Editor: Sarah Doughty
Designer: Malcolm Walker

First published in 1997 by
Wayland Publishers Ltd
61 Western Road, Hove
East Sussex BN3 1JD

Find Wayland on the internet at http://www.wayland.co.uk

British Library Cataloguing in Publication Data
Moses, Brian, 1950 –
"I don't care!" : learning about respect. – (Values)
1. Respect – Juvenile literature
I. Title II. Gordon, Mike, 1948 –
170

ISBN 0 7502 2093 7

Printed and bound by G. Canale & C.S.p.A.,
Turin

CONTENTS

What does respect mean?. 4

Other people care for us 6

Respect for what others do 8

Respect for opinions 10

Respect for feelings 11

Respect for privacy 12

Being considerate towards others . . .13

Respect for rules 14

Respect for animals 20

Respect for places we visit 22

Disrespectful people 24

Other people return our respect 26

Develop self-respect 28

Notes for parents and teachers 30

Books to read 31

Index .32

Respect can mean all kinds of things.

It can mean ... I admire your good qualities and, someday, I hope I can be like you too.

Usually we feel like this about our parents and our teachers.

Respect also means showing concern and consideration.

The way our parents and teachers care for us shows that they respect us.

They encourage us to do our best.

Go for it!

We can also respect people we don't know, people we've read about or seen on the television ...

We admire them for the
things they do.

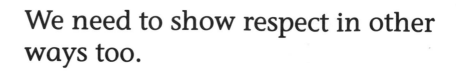

We need to show respect in other ways too.

We should always be ready to respect someone else's opinion.

Even though we don't agree with them we should still listen to what they have to say.

We need to respect other people's feelings.

If we don't, then we may say things that upset them.

We should also be ready to respect someone's privacy.

Boom Boom

If someone wants to be left alone, to think, to read quietly or just to relax, we need to be considerate.

So that we can all live together safely there have to be rules that everyone respects.

There are rules in the classroom, such as –

don't play with scissors ...

don't flick paint around
the room.

There are other places, too, where we need to be considerate and respect rules.

Perhaps there are rules in your local park on park notices –

no dogs.

... no skateboarding.

NO SKATEBOARDING

When we go on holiday and stay at a campsite there may be rules –

no noise after 10 pm.

18

When we use the library –

no eating.

We should
respect animals,
however small.

They all have a right
to life just as we do.

We need to show respect for the places we visit so that others can enjoy them too.

We don't want to walk around places where people have thrown away their rubbish.

Nor do we want to find graffiti
spoiling the places we visit.

Booooooooo

People who don't show respect
are said to be disrespectful.

Sometimes they are rude ...
being cheeky, making faces,
hissing or booing.

Sometimes they don't take care of other people's things.

If we show respect for others, we hope that they will consider us.

If we are concerned for others, we hope that they will show concern for us.

Perhaps the most important sort of respect that we need to develop is SELF-RESPECT.

This means that we have a feeling of pride in who we are and what we do.

We show respect to others by behaving in the right way and considering their needs.

NOTES FOR PARENTS AND TEACHERS

Read the book with children either individually or in groups. How often do children say 'I don't care' to someone? Think of situations where this kind of comment might be said. Do children really mean what they say? Talk about respect and how caring and concern for others is a big part of respect. How do adults show their concern for children? (It may well be interesting to look at notions of respectfulness under the rule of, e.g. Queen Victoria, when they believed that children should be seen and not heard. The poems of Robert Louis Stevenson may be of use here.)

How should children show their concern for other children? Can children draw up a list of ways to behave in the classroom or home when they are working or playing? They can start with the ideas in the book, e.g. try to respect other children's opinions, don't say things that we know will upset others, etc.

Children could be encouraged to write a story that shows the results of someone being disrespectful to others. Again some of the ideas in the book may prove useful starting points – breaking classroom rules, skateboarding in the park or taking a dog into the children's playground.

Why do we need rules? What would happen if there weren't any rules? Ask children to imagine the chaos that would result without any rules of the road. Encourage them to notice signs around the school and their environment. Note down what these signs say or draw them for a special display.

We all need to respect the rules in games too, whether it is a game of football or a board game. Without rules, anything would be allowed. Some children might like to devise their own board game and then try to draw up a list of rules. The game could then be given to other children to try out. Do the rules work?

Talk about vandalism. Reports of vandalism are only too easy to find in local papers each week. Make a collection of such reports and talk to the children about why vandalism takes place. Some children might like to act out a scene between a vandal who is intent on doing damage and an adult who has seen what is taking place.

Explore the notion of respect further through the sharing of picture books mentioned in the book list.

The above ideas will help satisfy a number of attainment targets in the National Curriculum Guidelines for English at Key Stage 1.

BOOKS TO READ

'*Long Neck and Thunder Foot*' by Helen Piers, illustrated by Michael Foreman (Picture Puffin, 1982)
A story of two dinosaurs who are frightened of each other at first but gradually learn to respect each other as individuals.

'*When Mum Turned Into A Monster*' by Joanna Harrison (Collins, 1996)
Two children show a lack of care and consideration for their mum and as the day goes on they fail to realize that their thoughtlessness is causing her to turn into a monster.

'*Something Else*' by Kathryn Cave & Chris Riddell (Picture Puffin, 1995)
Something Else is a small creature who has been rejected by everyone else until a creature called Something comes knocking at his door. They become friends and learn to respect each other's differences.

'*Sarah Scrap and Her Wonderful Heap*' by Wendy Lewis (Cloverleaf/Evans Brothers, 1990)
Sarah Scrap shows a group of children how to transform an area of wasteland in the middle of a town. Along the way they learn about respect for their environment.

'*A Child's Garden of Verses*' by Robert Louis Stevenson, illustrated by Brian Wildsmith (Oxford University Press)
These two poems are particularly useful in looking at behaviour in the past: '*Whole Duty of Children*' and '*Good and Bad Children*'.

INDEX

admiration 4, 9
animals, respect for
  20–21

care 25
concern 6
consideration 6, 26–7

encouragement 7

feelings 11

opinions 10

places, respect for 22–3
privacy 12

rudeness 24
rules 14–19

self-respect 28